JOE HILL MAKES HIS WAY INTO THE CASTLE

Katy Evans-Bush was born in New Y
of her life in London. Her blog *Baroque in Hackney* was short-
listed for the George Orwell Prize for political writing, and she
is currently working on a book about the new homelessness. She
now lives in Kent, where she is a freelance editor and poetry tutor.

also by Katy Evans-Bush

COLLECTIONS
Me and the Dead (Salt, 2008)
Egg Printing Explained (Salt, 2011)

PAMPHLETS
Oscar & Henry (Rack Press, 2010)
Broken Cities (Smith|Doorstop, 2017)

ESSAYS
Forgive the Language: Essays about Poetry and Poets
    (Penned in the Margins, 2015)

Joe Hill Makes His Way into the Castle

From lines by Kenneth Patchen

KATY EVANS-BUSH

 editions

First published in Great Britain in 2024
by CB editions
146 Percy Road London W12 9QL
www.cbeditions.com

Cover: Joseph S. Furey

Printed and bound in the UK by CMP Books

ISBN 978-1-909585-57-7

These things . . . but why only this!
Why do I stand here in this place with the whole sound
Of horror on my heart? What have I done
That I am separated from my kind?

– Kenneth Patchen

Contents

Preface ix

A note about Joe Hill xi

#1 'Ah, you puritan, you political zealot' 1

#2 'I don't know how the rest of you feel' 3

#3 'The corn really is as high as a dictator's eye' 4

#4 'This is not my idiolect' 5

#5 'I pick up the evening as dusk falls' 6

#6 *'& a thread snapped too soon'* 7

#7 'Thoughts & all the things you should have been doing' 8

#8 'The Bird Queen sits on a high branch' 9

#9 *'This man was my brother'* 10

#10 'Now is not the time' 11

#11 'On finding out that you have asked your landlord' 14

#12 'It was a bomby evening' 15

#13 'It wasn't much of a summer' 16

#14 'The origin of this, and this' 17

#15 'Oh, there's always another viewpoint' 18

#16 'O splendid to reach a craft & creed' 19

#17 'Rock-a-bye poor ladies' 20

#18 'I too am something of a stranger here' 21

#19 'I'm writing a letter to the country' 22

#20 'That old woman lost the toss' 23

#21 'The days of explosions were far from over' 24

#22 'Let's talk about the grown-up daughter' 25

#23 'The body of paper' 26

#24 'His front tooth is decaying' 27

#25 'There, at the entrance to the other world' 28

#26 'The Grand Palace of Versailles' 30

#27 'Last days of a wet, dying year' 32

#28 'A white kitchen sink' 33

#29 'Dear Mr Patchen' 35

#30 'The whisky wraps its duplicitous arms around me' 37

#31 'O great stuffed shirts of the BBC and the UN' 38

#32 'First, we are their products' 39

#33 'Walking muddleheaded in a muddled country' 41

#34 'No no no' 42

#35 'Portrait of the artist as a novel' 43

#36 'How little we cared before it was too late' 44

#37 'You'd be a ghost too' 45

#38 'Encounter at nightfall' 47

#39 'The business of redemption' 48

#40 'We were always so sure of ourselves' 50

#41 'O bird' 52

#42 *'The one we're really watching is Rishi Sunak'* 53

#43 'A fiend slays the children of the messenger' 55

#44 'So tired of all this pathos' 56

#45 'This darkness has lasted two months' 57

#46 'Days the anger leaves you' 58

#47 'Jo Hill makes his way into the castle' 59

#48 'This body of blood & flesh' 60

#49 .Some rooms you have to climb up out of' 61

#50 'Life!' 63

#51 'This town wakes up so early' 64

Source notes 66

Acknowledgements 71

Preface

The poet Kenneth Patchen was an important counterculture figure in the US. A defiantly working-class poet whose life spanned the first and second world wars, the Depression and Vietnam, he inspired the Beats (though his own drummer played a more austere beat than theirs). If Percy Shelley was right about poets being 'the unacknowledged legislators of the world', you could trust Patchen with the position. His poems are incantatory, exhortatory and passionate. They occupy a mythical space with an American tinge and a universal outlook. A romantic, he wrote about disillusionment. A pacifist, he wrote about war and the human condition of violence. I read Patchen voraciously in my teens, writing the titles of poems I liked on the inside cover. Half of them are called 'To Miriam'; Miriam was his wife, and he was a lover, not a fighter.

By the end of the 2021 lockdown I was in a bad state. I'd had a terrible time: unceremoniously displaced from gentrified London, homeless, then Covid, lockdown, Long Covid, months of solitude and the death of my pet bird. My lockdown companion. I couldn't write. And the world was beginning to reassert itself in new, horrific ways.

I needed help.

I thought of my friend Peter, who keeps an old toffee tin full of cut-out words for prompts. I thought I might try it myself. So I got out my broken old Collected Patchen, bought with baby-sitting money when I was 15; I hadn't read him in years. I'd already replaced it, I'd even used a few pages for birthday cards. I took the scissors to it. Lines, phrases, pieces of titles. I didn't read, I simply skimmed for what caught my eye. As I skimmed, it all came flooding back – Patchen's voice, his lexicon, his generosity, his challenges, his demands that we all try to be better. And found myself somehow flooding back to myself. I realised it was going to be a conversation – between me and Patchen, between me and poetry, between England-me and America-me, between rootless-cosmopolitan-me and the little town I'd washed up in.

I put the phrases into a round cardboard box which had originally held a chocolate praline wafer brought back by my best friend from that most beautiful and civilised establishment, E. Wedel of Warsaw. The Old World, the New World, the same old world.

To begin each poem I chose four or five phrases – very fast, like tarot cards, but face up – and laid them on my desk as stepping stones across the various enormities. Once used, they went into the lid of the box. Only very slowly did I dimly begin to see the obvious parallel between my situation now – alone in a small town where I arrived knowing no one – and at 16 when we had moved from our home city to a little old farming and industrial village on the Connecticut River.

Patchen himself lived in a personal lockdown of chronic pain, after one serious back injury in his twenties and then another. Bedridden in his last few years (he died at 60), still he was fully present, fully creative – even prolific – and his writing, drawings and paintings burst with his energy.

As I wrote, through political crises, yet more Covid and a close family bereavement, my physical and mental health were both suffering. I had no resilience except on the page. The poems grew darker. And the darker I wrote, the better I felt. And here we are. As this book goes to print, the world situation has darkened still further; my initial fears of the material beginning to feel dated were misplaced. Thus, as well as being like a diary, or a phone (as per #29), they're also like a map.

Most of Patchen's phrases have been kept, though many have been changed, cut, rearranged, or edited out. These poems couldn't exist without them – nor without that lost girl who sat writing and rewriting and rewriting her poems.

Joe Hill was a Swedish immigrant and union organiser for the IWW – the International Workers of the World, or Wobblies – in the days of America's labour struggle. The mine owners would call the Salvation Army in to drown out the workers' protests; Joe Hill wrote protest songs to the tunes of their hymns. We still sing them today. One of them, 'The Preacher and the Slave' (to the tune of 'In the Sweet By-and-By'), gave us the phrase 'pie in the sky', with its line, 'We'll get pie in the sky when we die'.

In Salt Lake City in 1915, Joe Hill was framed for a murder he didn't commit, and executed; campaigners for clemency included President Woodrow Wilson, the Swedish ambassador, and fellow IWW member Helen Keller. Before his execution Hill wrote to his IWW colleague Bill Heywood, 'Goodbye, Bill, I die like a true blue rebel. Don't waste any time mourning. Organize!' And then: 'Could you arrange to have my body hauled to the state line to be buried? I don't want to be found dead in Utah.' His last words were to the firing squad; as the commander gave them their orders – 'Ready! Aim!' – Hill interrupted to say, 'Fire – go on and fire!'

An estimated 30,000 people attended his funeral in Chicago. The song 'Joe Hill', written by Alfred Hayes in 1925 and set to music by Earl Robinson in 1936, has been recorded by many folk singers, and notably by Paul Robeson, and has ensured his continuing legacy.

From lines by Kenneth Patchen #1

Ah, you puritan, you political zealot, you religious zealot,
with your credo, your mindfulness, your anthology, you zealot
of cocktails, of running, of telling people what to think,
with your secret art-redefining event in a disused water-processing
plant on the outskirts of a town no one really lives in. Well –
no one you know. & you're such a lifeless, clever little
phony, you wouldn't really call that living.

You fake news, you fanatical suburbanite, you literalist,
you plodding proceduralist, you mildly racist structuralist, you
sexist whitist, you sexist even though you're a woman. You
materialist monolectician, you define yourself by your car
while the seawater rises around us, you think 'creativity'
is different from everything else, you buy coloured pens
to make mind maps of other people's ideas.

You think creativity is a different activity from everything else,
you clever, lifeless little coward, my little phony, you professional
partisan with no ideas; you think restlessness is energy.
Look around you: those leaves attached to the trees, so casual,
but pummelled see-through by the witlessly conventional wind.
& those striving engines that force the numberless wheels
to spin. Just noise! Do you think they know what they're doing?

You tired, sad, bedtime little phony, you namby-pamby,
fake reader, you're terrified of caring! Worse, you're terrified
of seeming to care. But that ball you set in motion just rolls faster
the further it goes down that hill, & at the bottom of that hill,
at the very bottom, is the real, the genuine you, the one
who was born with nothing to do but care, it was all you had,
caring & crying & milk, learning to see your own reflection,

& you had nothing to do but cling to your mother, you charlatan,
you coward baby, you name-calling egotist, because your mother
was real & she was milk, & sleep because sleep is real, & learn
to be real because that was the only way forward, the only way
a baby can grow, & learn to tell the difference because only real people
can teach you, you somnambulist; your spine & your head were both
straighter then. That's what it was like before, before all this deciding.

From lines by Kenneth Patchen #2

I don't know how the rest of you feel, these days
when the sky is pink & the trees are yellow
& the animals, all the animals, are blue. All I know
is that the birds, these great birds have seen us through
so far – & we sit in our chairs, we sit in our cars
& watch TV as their numbers come up. In this crumbling
black-mooned month in a time when water is air
& air is smoke, we cannot be happy with bluepinkyellow,
we must gather our wits, be slow, look for tripwires,
potholes, glue. Fuck your bunting; all is to play for.
I hear it said, & I say it doesn't matter, that time is not
real. You don't stop to think in a crumbling thoroughfare.
I say we must be green. Let it be showtime again.

From lines by Kenneth Patchen #3

That corn really is as high as a dictator's eye.
I had a book from the 1940s & it sang nigh-
falutin. O yes. It talked about *all the Nations*, but I
couldn't believe a word of it. Not now. We've seen
what happened next & there's no antidote, no amulet,
no way to prevent being charmed. Outside, the sun
is shining & I can hear some talking, a little plane,
children playing: a pretty hubbub. We've seen what people can do.

Yesterday they tried, we knew it wouldn't take long:
they tried to untell the untrue fairy story, but they only
made it more so. We eat ourselves. Bombs body parts blood,
dead children & dead soldiers. Nothing new can be told.
Nation of Nations swears revenge. Shush babies,
we'll sing you a little cannibal's bedtimesong.

From lines by Kenneth Patchen #4

This is not my idiolect. This is not my moment.
Borrowing the clothes of another emperor,
another time, I slink out invisibly into the fray.
Together [if this will place them better]
they weigh three hundred pounds [of pure explosive].
And it *is* a fray. With his quiet hands in his unquiet time,
I mean with his unquiet mind upon my hands,
I can think a little better about what to say.
Well, the grass is a pleasant thing. It is summer
after all. This awful dark summer brightness,
the same one that shines on all the atrocities,
all the Guernicas, all the grubby murders. The sun,
that old Switzerland, shines even on Kabul. We must
keep watch instead for the strange, moving lights of people.

From lines by Kenneth Patchen #5

I pick up the evening as dusk falls, pick up fidgets
as the storm hits. Here's a letter about the weather
to all you so-called liberals. Goddamn us all & our
carefully sorted recycling, & the freezer's friendly hum,

our ice-makers & our accounts at H&M.
We hate the frackers & we run our mouths off
on their hot old gas. It should be sufficient, what's
in front of us, food in the cupboard and garden,

the friends we live [if we're lucky enough] among.
But here I am, peering over thousands of miles
to a webcam, *again,* watching another hurricane.
Mom? It's just a street. You can't see anything really.

A webcam won't show you your mother, your friend,
or Dorothy. You have no magic powers. Goddamn us
with our throwaway utensils, joke presents, foil balloons,
goddamn our future. What we use is already rubbish.

Goddamn our frets, our ennui, our dissatisfaction.
Going on goddamn trips & calling it 'staycation'.
Marvels! We live scattered. Friends are everywhere:
under water, breathing smoke. We sit alone in our rooms.

We built this disembodied world, this loneliness,
we made the weather angry, we dug these holes in the ground,
we pulled the dinosaurs' ether into pipes & turned it into
the fusspot flame under last night's so-so supper.

Life itself should be the miracle! We house the spirits
of a thousand sermonising Lutherans in the bodies of the
Genghises, the Carnegies – the Gates of Hell. Goddamn our
empty words, our plastic applicators. No one will save us.

From lines by Kenneth Patchen #6

& a thread snapped too soon – why does this even make any kind of sense – threads don't come with a lifespan but I guess we tend to measure everything against us, especially when everything's against us – it's a joke, anyway – *Time*, they'd say – *what's time to a pig?* – but somehow this sewing analogy happens, the thread is done before the seam is, or the hem is, & you are falling a bit round the edge – & you keep saying to yourself, *Beautiful*, oh the pig's apple, the more it shrivels the sweeter it is, the more it wrinkles the more it has a face – hungry pig – sun going down, depth of its colour, rashness of its promises, the face of the apple – *Beautiful you are*, you say again as the owl himself strums & sings on his innocent little moonlit guitar – feathers for picks, horses for courses, the thread has snapped untimely tho & somehow you are still wearing the same dress

From lines by Kenneth Patchen #7

Thoughts & all the things you should have been doing
throng like shadowy caresses on a horizon
like trees through a brain fog, waving with abandon
the same white flag – is it snow, or surrender? Is it
you who'll surrender first, or them? Your enemies
obscured. Do me that love, I want to beg, *Be words* –
as the blossoms, yes blossoms! float to the ground like thoughts
& the list grows as your voice whitely whispers.

From lines by Kenneth Patchen #8

for Tiffany

The Bird Queen sits on a high branch,
a dancer, green & black, & down in the lone valley
the hero of the story, playing deeply in a glade,
consults the snowglobe in her brain. That's you.
The Bird Queen watches, totally focused,
with eyes like polished marbles.
She holds you among her feathers as she holds
the little girl in the snowglobe-brain she sits in.
The Bird Queen's fine. It's you who's in a tangle.
Don't presume to ruffle her, she'll give you the beak.
She is amused by your little fingers; the trees,
the mountains are her arms. Leaves rustle silver around her
& there is no other sound besides what she can hear.
if you slowed her song it would be the Song
of Solomon, the Song of the Shirt, the tale
of the horse who drinks. *Shhh!* She's about to speak . . .

From lines by Kenneth Patchen #9

This man was my brother. You sound
so true it has to be fake – we all know
you can lead a horse to slaughter –
that metaphor's stone-dead to the point

I have to wonder what a meta's for.
Srsly just look at him. That T-shirt,
that spiky hair, the trainers on his feet –
the terror in his eyes.

Oh wait, your brother never had that. Well,
in these days we confront the sadness
as best we can. It is pleasing to death for us
to be tired of being alive. Your *brother* – whatever

form the trouble was going to take he was still
trying to deal with it then. He wanted to eat the world,
its every prospect so utterly nourishing;
the times so expansive, so nearly possible.

Twenty years of it. He was your big brother.
You had the same smile. You laughed together
at his jokes, I mean at your jokes;
you ate his mother's cooking,

you finished his sentences. He's finishing
your sentence now. You knew you were
the favourite & so did he. Let's talk about Ahmed's
sister, his wife. *My sister,* you said – *my wife –*

No, no. Of course you didn't. Nevertheless,
they're here. This continual ministry of anger
must be all that feeds you now. You have his eyes,
you are his eyes now so try to see *her.*

From lines by Kenneth Patchen #10

> *Suddenly*
> *We knew that we could not belong again to simple love.*
> – Kenneth Patchen, 'In Judgement of the Leaf'

NOTE: This poem is constructed of a small percentage of the comments I saw on social media saying why people shouldn't be protesting. Lines in italics are by either Kenneth Patchen or me.

Now is not the time. I thoroughly
support BLM, but Covid has crystallised
the need for respect. Especially at this time.

It's a tricky one but
on the one hand you can't sanitise history –
of course it is great to see so many people
out supporting Black Lives Matter. But!
It's a tough one. Protest, to be effective,
needs an element of self-restraint.
Marxists and anarchists. They are social terrorists.
The government should take control and put
a stop to the blatant lack of social distancing.
Very conflicted. There is a pandemic on?
There's no doubt that the statue isn't appropriate, but
I'm not mad about stuff being destroyed.

Say! It's beginning to rain, she said, and these cretins
think this is the way to make a point? It's a bad sign
and I'm sorry if that makes me an idiot.
I think some people's concern is where will this end?

Now is not the time for protest. It's not,
it's not much to grow wings over, she said.
When lockdown is lifted we will all have plenty
of opportunity. Not a bunch of yobs.

Where is the line drawn? What will make it better?
Do all the Germans want the death camps removed?
And don't forget the economic crisis.

The whole thing is endless narcissism.
That said OF COURSE it's not to dismiss the reality
of racism. There are some people out there
that don't care if this pandemic is ever over.
Where is the dignity, where are the thoughtful speeches?

Can't help but wonder. Respect for our police –
our heritage and tradition, however flawed
it was *[however flawed]*. Distract, divide.
When was the consultation on this issue?
Maybe start a petition? Extremism always
creates resentment. I have tried to convince
BLM activists to move away from physical
protests and to go online. I'm not at all conflicted.

Very tough choice. The issue is tangled, complex.
We were most prominent in having slavery abolished.
Will the whole of Liverpool be pulled down?
'Protests.' Well I am sick of them. I would also like to see
more statues of women like that of Nancy Astor.

I think we have to be very, very careful.
The government know the protesters are angry
so what are you expecting them to do.
Waiting for vandalistic mobs to flout
the rules of law – the leftist assault on Britain –
On the other hand do they
not know we have a democratic process
for dealing with these issues? It is war.

It unacceptable and an insult to the memory
of George Floyd

[& Mark Duggan, & Joy Gardner,
& Jean Charles de Menezes, & Stephen Lawrence,
& Joe Hill says let them burn us, hang us, shoot us,
because they grew tired of all the common mysteries,
because the sky was too beautiful for them
to stand it, because it's only by standing together
listening to the words of a guy named Freedom,
that we have what it takes to make songs with].

This puts people's backs up and achieves nothing.
I personally think this can be dealt with properly,
negotiated in a civilised way.
Maybe someone should offer an alternative
way to air these grievances and anger
in the context of these times [*Now is not it*].
It's self-defeating. When the pandemic is over.
And on and on we go, forever and ever.

From lines by Kenneth Patchen #11

On finding out that you have asked your landlord
to replace the ancient heaters in your flat
the day before the studio flat next door
is let for £60 a month more than you're paying.

The danger of appearing to be demanding,
the danger of appearing. Appearing cold.
The danger of the new tenancy agreement,
at any rent, whenever he wants to send it.

Harrowed by these apprehensions, I resolved
to commit myself to the mercy of the storm.
The agency, too, will be wanting their commission.
Our forms of knowledge are ever incomplete.

I can't understand! Joe Hill listens to the people
while your landlord, alive as you or me, whacks
the top of an egg. His wife pours out the tea.
You may stay no longer in a place

than the permit for your dreamscape;
gather only that which you can carry yourself.
Already it's too much. Jettison, jettison.
Books, furniture, the idea of being warm.

I can't understand! While all around, the towns,
the groves & bogs, the thorns & brakes, the creeks
[*'There are no losses. There is only life'*]
& the marshes all sit quiet through the night.

From lines by Kenneth Patchen #12

It was a bomby evening, & the stars
watched intently over the camp of tents:

495,000 years pouring into the museums
of science & this is all we really meant.

Bring on their cannon and iron sugar, brother,
for all the culture in the world won't make us wonderful.

A leaf like a pennant waves over the scene
& passes his own green judgement on it

[sirens & stretchers] not that anyone asked him for it;
he is the spirit [blood on the walls] of Noplace.

All these histories of those who stood outside it:
You can't make a fatherland out of a butcher shop,

so this is all we know, the rags of satchels,
the various howling cells we have lovingly spawned.

You may all go home now. The TV cameras leave.
A little girl holds out her hand. *That'll be twenty cents.*

From lines by Kenneth Patchen #13

It wasn't much of a summer. You could as well
write the biography of the northern rain as sit
on a deck chair in a sweeping expanse. All the flowery
talk, the magical mouse, the screen for company
& the house, the house, the house, the lack of a house;
that lute in the attic sat silent these three hundred years.
It has no dimensions left, but still at night you can vaguely
make out its little airs. Something once plucked those strings.
Two ghosts together, we sit, & it's for me, the living,
to make some music here in this attic. It wasn't much of a summer,
but I did manage to pick up on a few things.

From lines by Kenneth Patchen #14

The origin of this, and this, about which we know nothing,
becomes its own folkloric meaning & open to interpretation,

thus nothing. We are a mystery to our own mothers. That isn't
politics. The origin we understand, though not sportsmen ourselves.

Luckily we can predict what our machine guns will do. Our comfort
     now
is how white & still the hours before they deliver all the others

unto our only remaining cathedral – & our eternity goes sliding
down the hills. All our home runs, our grandparents' heroes, our
     foregoing

pennants & Joe diMaggios & ritual seasons. Fighter or not, the one
rule seems to be: you must meet the stick with your willing body.

From lines by Kenneth Patchen #15

Oh, there's always another viewpoint.
Take that leaf,
for example: the way it
dangles
on that tree. It sits
in judgement on what it sees; there is
this commonality
                    between us & it.
But the autumn leaf is emblazoned
                    with spring's belief.
A man lives down here, a man with a
spade in his head. His name is Doug.
                    Doug dug a dugout
one day down where the leaf can't see –
home for himself
                    & for the wretched
skeleton on the rock
                    who only sits
& thinks *rock*.
                    Meanwhile the middle
class was sitting on its fat
paid-for sofa thinking – well, we know
what they're
what we're
                    thinking.
The body of the living beats in my hand:
perennial & schemeless.

From lines by Kenneth Patchen #16

O splendid to reach a craft & creed:
the words flowing freely, yes!
A thinking book on a white IKEA table.
& I had it neatly written, too –
my winter poem on the first of September,
in a slant of sunshine, or what looked like it –

but I couldn't stop thinking about how old
the world is, & how beautiful every particle,
even hidden somewhere in the evil,
& this led me far from where
I wanted to be. I had finished my dinner,
my plate of steaming fish, & gone for a walk.
When I came back it was twenty years later,
& where were my beautiful words?

From lines by Kenneth Patchen #17

Rock-a-bye poor ladies, the world was ever cruel & wrong.
This time it goes down singing a cruel cowboy song:
there's a pretty little lady in the State of the Lone Star,
in a state of do & re-do, & she'll have to travel far,

& her heart is cold as clay, in a cloud of white linen,
& her heart is hard as clay, for the state says she's sinnin' –
but 'sin' is a form of moral threat & has no place in law.
Her heart is cracked as clay. & she can't travel. She's poor.

Your problem is one of sex, says Man in Stetson Hat, who has none.
She thinks, *that's funny enough to break my heart, if I still had one*,
but the blood's been drained away from it & she knows she's alone.
She sings, *Boxers always hit harder when there are women around.*

There's a bounty-hunter keeping watch to sue whoever helps her –
she must speak in code for 'transport', 'money', 'blood', & 'shelter'.
You can sit down & listen, but she'll keep her story short,
because anyone who sympathises with her could end up in court

– & the thing about a civil suit is, it keeps the state clean.
It's divide-&-conquer, it's dirty tricks, it's the sub-routine,
It's informers, it's Stasi, it's the shame of the county,
& no man's life can be beautiful if even one man gets this bounty.

O Lady, poor lady, please sit pretty tight
while help's smuggled in by stealth of night –
too late for you, maybe, but maybe not too late for your sister –
tell her, *just sit tight till the soul plasma gets here.*

You're just a young lady in the backstreets of Laredo,
O young lady in Laredo, with your life still ahead –
But this re-do is a no-do, & your coat-hanger's waiting –
& this law will still be working if you wind up dead.

From lines by Kenneth Patchen #18

I too am something of a stranger here, my friend. We talk
of others who appear so much a part of it, we say,
collected – failing to consider that the act itself, each day
is just an ongoing striving collation, every morning
a decision: the correct accessories for that day's gather.
Now if you go for a walk. It's a smallworld. It's the pitcher of life,
drink it. Your milk. A path, a rotting boat of spines, the church
spire a needleprick that pulls the clouds, ruffles the sky.

The sun is setting & you finally know what mind
your mind's been wearing all day besides these coils of wet
tangled hair. Taking courage – yes – from the splendid
orange mess, & alive, you stride on, womanfully strange
for once, & this is your own collected town, & you are
a man: they'll love you, you'll see [when you find them].

From lines by Kenneth Patchen #19

I'm writing a letter to the country [it doesn't
matter which one]. Dear country, this is to say please
open the window! There's no fresh air, & you are
stale & enervated. You're suffering beach poisoning,
shit poisoning, hate poisoning. When you shrink
we all lose strength, dear Country, & you know it.
You've pulled your knife to try & be the tough, but
you haven't looked what's down your enemies' socks.

This is my letter: Dear Old Men [you don't know
who you are but everybody else does]: you've betrayed
your living animal into hands more cruel & bloody
than your own. Open the window! Nobody here can breathe,
no one dares make a sound, & your breath stinks
of rotten meat, hypocrisy, & rusted crowns.

From lines by Kenneth Patchen #20

That old woman lost the toss.
She stood in the market square,
calculated her loss
& her unsustainable care;

she pondered being shelterless
& stood in a strange light.
She thought, *I'll be all right.*
She had no choice.

I saw a different thing there:
the common ardour of most
for the common gains: fear,
 denial of helplessness,

faith in the crumbled House.
The fall still follows pride:
it's the old tired fight.
Nothing is any use.

As the woman stood alone,
& wondered what to try,
the unimaginable moon
continued to look away.

The days of explosions were far from over but
        you filled your sack with
tiger cubs! We were thus far so nobly advanced
they didn't even bite! Fields of earth, red wine:
the question was, who is afraid of what?
But peace is only manifold fusions, I mean
carefully folded & striped illusions.
Thus far so nobly advanced are we
you can't take your chances anywhere.
Though come & take me down the allotment
to stand by the millgates, the old wheels.
How they turned! The ducks who circle around the pond
        so flocculent & apparently real
are no more present than you or me.

Lines From Kenneth Patchen #22

Let's talk about the grown-up daughter
of Cinderella, & the fuss she nearly made
one morning, standing on a parapet.
Yes! She wasn't asking for very much.
Precisely she was asking for less, less, less

of everything. Less lace, less fuss, less silk,
less carriage. She was hungry for the raw
world. She'd never seen it. She dreamed of it
every night, the sheer physicality of it:
mould, weather, metal zips, bad sex, work.
It was the rain, a rogue star, the snow,
the *cold* that got her. She fretted at her book:

Dostoyevsky. Why oh why could she not
meet a man like that, instead of these egotistical
princes with their haircuts. What a thought:
a man who'd pawn his own wife's frying pan;
she'd never known a person take anything that seriously.

She'd tease him about it while she boiled the eggs.
Together they would find real things to sanctify.
Real sentences, & pumpkins. She'd make soup.
He would write all day & she would work
on her thesis. & on the fried-egg mornings
they'd be so hungover, so covered with the soot –

From lines by Kenneth Patchen #23

The body of paper
lives between the pages of a book

like a star pressed into a child's hand
its different parts marked in dotted lines

white as a page
it's seen its own ghost

there is no hand
and what after all are words

From lines by Kenneth Patchen #24

His front tooth is decaying. It feels
hollow inside, like a cartoon
undersea grotto. The light

is eerie but the line, the drawing
is uninspired. It's all
enthusiasm. It eats away

substance. Meanwhile elsewhere:
a tooth at a time he's becoming
obsolete as the poet's skylark.

That pandemic dream of extinction.
A brick thrown under the wheel,
a microplastic fairy-wing.

A visit from the toothgrinder.
He brushes his teeth with red wine –
kills eternity by injuring an hour –

the bite of its mist on his brain.
He is become Spongebob.
Toothless Plankton has a word but

That depends on whose science,
he says, *Sonny Boy. Keep talking,*
these holes have got all day.

From lines by Kenneth Patchen #25

There, at the entrance to the other world,
every prospect looked tired.
He wanted to throw something
so he picked up a baseball.
It looked tired. The world, it said
, is too old. Too old for a home
run, it said, & added
you can't run home.
Though that never
stopped anybody trying.
Whatever home is. Do you know, Mister?

No one knows what's important any more,
not here at the border
with the underworld where there is
no currency that's valid.
There's only what
was always important
[This he knew without being told]
& & & AND.
The rest [he told the ball, looking
right in its limp
stitches] *is nonsense
& treason*. Just ask
the millions who wait without light.

There at the entrance to another world
he looked at the sea of bodies
& thought to himself,
They look tired. & with that
he threw the old tired baseball up
into the air, the last air,
the air before the end,
where it ascended

& ascended & never came down
as long as he kept looking.
It was the last full
measure of devotion.

From lines by Kenneth Patchen #26

The Grand Palace of Versailles:
what a microcosm of trickle-down!

No art of any form by any means
by recording or by electronic sampling or
by carving or chiselling or by looking

or carefully listening or by any means at all
can resist the pull of money.
See the pious patrons down here in the corner.

The sense of command has ever
[*You're fired!*] been reached
& power needs mostly nothing
to take over   [Chaos!]   quick,
join hands & don't create a vacuum!

Elements in a harmonious state would slot in alongside.
Apartments & little houses would lean

on each other's shoulders & sleep
& the grass would breathe through
the delicate night & the earth underneath.

Every pen every paintbrush every pixel
contains the world & each
molecule follows its own trajectory.

Think of all those workshops
buzzing think of all those little
flowers of phosphorus.

Men in silk handing over bags of coins.
The skilled creators of beauty hard at work.
Their children's dinner.

From lines by Kenneth Patchen #27

Last days of a wet, dying year & we're
peering over the edge. If nobody's sick,
you weren't really there – it's the swinging
sixties again but without, without the
optimism. The edge of what, you ask. Hit me,
hit me, hit me over, hit me over, hit me over
those white, those white cliffs of Dover
& watch me fall. But let the birds – I say,
shut the curtains, I wish you had no look-in here,
Mr Death. I made a pledge, I prayed a prayer,
but you got the upper hand. Jesus, though.
We thought it was a pretty world before.

From lines by Kenneth Patchen #28

for Mary Evans & Tom Vink-Lainas, i.m.

A white kitchen sink   wall of old tools
row of teapots   bellyful of leaves
that read themselves   in the night
Dead forests now   where Mary once stood

Among the frogs and   puritans
us misfits   'intellectuals'
all is whispered   witches
we tried to be good enough
We all did   and we all were

The stories go down the centuries
Louisa   kids in the back
of that covered wagon again
get-away   get-away across the plains
& then that train   beer
baseball game   Kansas sun
Great-great-granddad never stood a chance
& a ball still   arcs across that sky
such an unreal blue

Funny how you die and still persist
                              We all do

Something in the pot   Tom's turkey soup
Out the window   his dry stone walls
the well   the even better
This isn't some *auld lang*
                              Oh yes it is

that wall of tools was the birthright I tell you
Paintbrushes   drumsticks

books & pictures & Mary
like the gun in Chekhov's hall they must be used

Two old aunts returned like a parcel
to Tartu to the   old house to the old
fugitive kiss of   the sky's delirium

Bye said Tom   and the years
floated back like clouds
circus in the sky unfunny circus
Bye Daddy   *Bye little man*
said Daddy standing at the dock

I'll cirrus in my dreams

I'm assuming that in the world he will always be
with us one way   or another and I hope
that's ok with Tom I loved him right from the

Oh Mary Mary you   little chickerbug
You are our   our only
shine, you make us
in there   somewhere, honey
The pavements sing where once Mary stood

From lines by Kenneth Patchen #29

Dear Mr Patchen,
                    Look back, look back.
See that kid. That little town, with its granite, its bare
birches & maples everywhere perpendicular,
snow lying crisp as a shirt, & the beautiful
curl-cracking cold on the morning walks to school.
A row of stores on Main Street I can't remember,
a disused machete factory down by the river,
& cars full of kids driving fast down shadowy roads
where the sky was impasto-thick on a dark night.
These cars were a death-cult and the woods
rustled, too dense to see through with Indian ghosts.
See that fat, serious black-&-white book she read,
and see your serious, trustworthy profile on it.
Look, you said to that little weirdo.
You have a life – use it! She asked you then:
Have you by any chance change
for one hundred and ninety dullards, sir?
She knew she was dullards one to a hundred.
We must grow up into our wits as we go
and never stop trying.
                            Now in a very different little town
I'm handing you a tin can, Ken. Punctured
with a length of knotted string. I'm holding it out
across the decades – it was a very popular toy –
and here in a present that loops back through another
kind of past I hold a can of my own.
In this place, all has been written and all has been
absorbed: the place is layered like a Rothko
with explosions, orchards, nuns, brewers, dogs,
Romans, & I've run out of words. Come on, Mister –
help a girl out of a jam. I'm using your poems,
if you don't mind, like a phone. Hold the string taut.
You're doing the talking. I'm taking notes.

Then I'm doing the talking and you took the notes.
On alternating levels the world pounds in,
its colours unravelled, its people unpredictable,
and our string is frayed! The scene is indistinct.
It has been written and how can it be unwritten?
Be an eye, you say. We have to be alive
to every minute we're here.

                          Hate and fear O blast
the rest of it to hell – *& just write*, you say.

From lines by Kenneth Patchen #30

The whisky wraps its duplicitous arms around me;
I always pull at a party and this one's just the whisky
& Robert Burns & me. Every day is the end of days
these days, & today we're glued to the news

as always. & especially to the news that stayed news,
circa 1795. Round & round & round we go,
disaster after disaster. *A man's a man for a' that*
Robbie knows, & I sing along, but what never changes:

The truth is always the thing they won't say.
Sure there's still food, if you know where to get it:
the food bank. Queue of 80. My friend
stood ages out there the other day in that cold

that frosts the children & grandmas, & once again
Mr Burns I'm feeling guilty to celebrate your day
with a pile of neeps & tatties, a little haggis,
a fifth of something warming, and your song.

We're counting to that day when we can watch it fall –
all of it, fall. Fall in a tottering sparkle
out in the street & on TV. We all need something
different to happen. Showers of light.

So tonight I'm here with the news on and it might
be something. This early day, because you can only
begin from where you are, is the day to drink the whisky
& let the police, yes, investigate the government.

From lines by Kenneth Patchen #31

O great stuffed shirts of the BBC & the UN,
O great Russian Delegate & Parley a mentarian,
your faces are none the redder for what happened there
as you lie your arses off in front of the world,

& with all nations sitting represented in the same
great meeting room, or television studio,
or living room that you desecrate with your dead eyes,
anybody's ordinary room with its central heating & tea tray

& the dog curled up beside them on the couch,
anybody's living womb, or bad luck! anybody's
dying room where a shell could so easily make a new
window simply by coming in, & with the world

all watching – those who are, I mean, those who aren't
slathering their bullshit into a pint glass or into their
wife's left eye – we don't have to watch you to get
the gist of the lies you tell, your great dessicating lies

of patriarchy plutocracy money & death: what do I have
to say to you? There is nothing to say. This is my town!
That was our human town. Handful of broken pots
and scattered   [*footnote for newsreel*]

From lines by Kenneth Patchen #32

First, we are their products.
We grow up in their houses. Before we can
begin to be the future we are put to sleep
in the grey & gentle cradle of the past:
we rest in its betrayals & its dust,
we look for several years through its windows,
part its heavy curtains, its musty blinds,
trail our hands along its varnished banisters.
We must be slow. Only once we've felt all this
boredom, once we've been formed by what
their parents left to them, & theirs to them,
can we hurtle forward to be the promise of
the future & push our blue cart into the water.

But oh, the ones we raise! Our mighty atoms,
they're born already the future, we can see it
& we feel the energy of their force fields.
It takes so many years to see they're only
like we are, like we were – that they too
are made of what our parents & grandparents did.
They have to make their graffiti on our walls,
wreck our dusty curtains, trample our flowers
before they can go out & spread their shine
In ways we never dreamed would be the ways.

The very unlucky of us live too long
and see our children's decline – their failing health,
falling hair, their dental plates & divorces,
botched careers & arthritis – & die worrying.
We are all, always & only, all of us children
& the promise we are given is always broken,
but what a promise! & so we love each other.
Each generation tries to break the chain
& clear the way for the new world to begin

according to our intentions & our wishes.
If only we could see it. Little meteors,
how mighty we are & how we could be perfect.

From lines by Kenneth Patchen #33

Waking muddleheaded in a muddled country
& now the train is slowing down.
You're not on a train. The vines with their tendrils
like railway ties have finally caught up with you –
Triffids, nothing but them is moving, & you have lost
your wheelie case & thus your laptop too. You haven't
so much *lost* it as it's disappeared by itself
with its wheels & handle & little white polka-
dots. In truth you had donated it to the char-
ity shop months ago when the lockdown ended,
but right now it's missing with the means of your live-
lihood in it & you find that you are barefoot.
There is an enclave of some sort. You follow the
strange unaccustomed moving lights of people. Going in, you find it warm, built of wood, there's a fire,
& people are lounging or standing around, playing violins & other things, a mandolin
maybe, & singing. Backcountry Blues. Your bare
feet draw attention. An old man says, Where's your bag?
They get a posse up to go find it, which you know
they never will. It's gone. You won't stay. You have to walk
home barefoot. Someone offers you a coat, a big man's
coat, & then you realise how cold you really are.
Then you wake up in the muddled country. Your laptop is on the table but somehow what remains
is the missingness of that ugly little navy
blue wheelie case with its catalogue lady dots & its
wobbly handle which has disappeared, & those
railway tracks made of twisting vines stretching out
into the middle of nowhere. Really nowhere.

No no no Oh we here we are living out our
little pretend lives drinking our beer feeling
bored or annoyed no no the pandemic the
three-storey lockdowns with wine and jig-
saws and too much Amazon piss off you
old men with all your paranoid answers no
don't you come to me chatting your facile
self-satis-

                    no I said
Oh it's easy to say god knows it's easy to say
it's so cheap with all the recipes & holidays
& the world is getting pretty dark if you ask
me but you don't you are a warship & there
is nothing to say to you so just fuck off go
& watch your Chomsky on youtube & opine
about conspiracies на хуй знов I said на хуй

From lines by Kenneth Patchen #35

Portrait of the artist as a novel
Portrait of the artist as a young gull
Portrait of the artist as a novel with no plot
Portrait of the artist as chocolate, as diamante, as ice
Portrait of the artist in chapter one where a seagull stares at a chip
Portrait of the artist as a passenger, call it steerage, but no one is steering
Portrait of the artist as a stowaway, as there is no hastily packed suitcase like a book, so
                    stick it up your frigate to bear you worlds away

Portrait of the artist as Guernica
Portrait of the artist in the style of Goya
Portrait of the artist as a passenger pigeon
Portrait of the artist with 173 tattoos, all of them on the inside
Portrait of the artist as a frigate full of hastily packed suitcases
Portrait of the artist as a passive watcher of television news with a fully paid-up licence
Portrait of the artist as a burlap sack full of seeds that can never be transported to the only
places where they could ever grow because those places don't exist any more & anyway
              there was never any such thing as a safe passage

43

From lines by Kenneth Patchen #36

How little we cared before it was too late!
Our city's hollow underneath the streets.
The parks are owned by private corporations,
the walls have spikes so the homeless can't sleep
and all of us are living out on the very edge.
The rich keep private towns under their houses.
Their hands are on the latches of our doors
and we are sick with the dirt of their money.
No scrubbing will get us clean of the spores.
Oh, I'll come and get you in a taxi, honey;
Or would've, back when we could afford a taxi.

From lines by Kenneth Patchen #37

You'd be a ghost too
                Worn to a stub

Expectoplasm
                A thing of the past

Don't touch a thing
                Oh wait it can't

It's a Zen thing
                About opening up

Examining yourself
                Then turning the volume

Down, if you're lucky
                No, keep turning

Or is it about finding
                Everybody else wanting

You look & you look
                Try to fix it in your mind

Establish its veracity
                Prove yourself sentient

We'll all be dead after while
                But there's always

One detail not right
                War, frankly

We keep thinking about this
        We fret about *empathy*

We worry away our own
        Substance on the barbed wire

Booby traps
        Shreds of our former

Selves hanging off them
        An arrangement in white and grey

Mossy red
        We can't tell what's beautiful any more

& we feel nothing
        Behind our faces

From lines by Kenneth Patchen #38

Encounter at nightfall, atmospheric with candles –
a black book, songs sung by serious men in an old language,
redemption peddled by stick, by habit, by blind faith,
its little flames glinting gold off the guilt – come again?
Women & children behave as they must in the face of
all that raw power. Why cavil that terms are less than civil,

if the cake sale's cancelled? I can't handle all this holiness.
these empires. As a formula for life it's more like death.
As an exculpation of death it looks too much something
they have invented for themselves with their feeble imaginations –
& as a moral code it's something more like kindergarten.

What are these stories? Are they for self-justification,
& only when we think we're caught? Is this really
the best we can do? We're evil. Human beings everywhere
are bathed in blood & your conscience is smeared with it same as mine.
We might as well be turned inside out, for all the good
piety does us, for all the waterproofing we get of it.

They carve each other up, while they carve *us* up:
men's hands behind their backs, women naked & burnt
to hide the first crime. Who got off lightly there? No one.
Make those eggs devilled. & when the soldiers finally break through
into the City of Mary, & they always do break through to this city,
we'll wish our Mary'd been mother to a vengeful god.

From lines by Kenneth Patchen #39

This business of redemption. We are pretty
animals with exactly the delusions
to imagine that all of nature's tuned to the melody
of some ancient song of our own devising.
But what makes us worthwhile?

You mention Dostoyevsky,
who made a new redemption for himself.
He suffered such lacerations that he became
a sort of monster. But he saw beauty everywhere,
except the places where we look for it.

I mention Mozart:
how could you listen to *Cosi Fan Tutte*
& not be better than you were before it?

Others mention Jesus
& say that he redeems the smallest of us
literally in the heartbeat of a sparrow.
Such strange beauty, hanging under a tree
like the fruit of the knowledge of good & evil.

Julian of Norwich had herself bricked up
in a little cell away from the world,
temptation & the sinful corruption of being
an ordinary person. Just *of being.*
But what did she achieve? That *all shall be well,*
& *all manner of things shall be well?*
Could she not have been good and not a cell?
If good exists only as a response,
was it ever any good? Where do we find
a single scrap of evidence
that 'goodness' conquers anything at all?

Think of the Crusades:
how Arab doctors taught their medicine
to the semi-civilised, bloodsoaked zealots
who'd butchered them, & saved the lives of countless –
that's us – along with their innocent own.
Hacked to pieces in the name of the same
lamb of God. Was this redemption?

As children, out in the back yard in summer,
we used to kill ants by pouring boiling water
down the ant hills, boiling their food, their families,
their beautiful cities, their intelligent faces.
I don't even remember why we did it.
Wouldn't you bite us, if you were an ant?

The Universe is a whimsical confection
and Philip Johnson is the celestial architect:
all our philosophy's a piece
of ersatz Chippendale.

Our brains can't wrap themselves around its size,
the shapes & features that we've given it,
its predilection for gratuitous
ornamentation. One thing
we tell ourselves makes life more manageable:
Beauty is what's seen from far away.

As for the fruit of the knowledge of good & evil,
Some primitive sign will be the most that we
can muster of our animality, our humility.
Art's not redemption. Art's just how we're tuned.

From lines by Kenneth Patchen #40

We were always so sure of ourselves.
We had something they didn't have,

the warmongers, the old men left over
from last time, so very sure of themselves,

who had dropped the bomb, won the war.
It was enough for us to be innocent –

we held the upper hand, we had no suit
with the common mysteries of our own

human nature. As if there is only one war
anywhere, the unjust war, & all you had to do

was stand in front of a tank holding a flower.
As if we didn't know what *they* do to people

who stand in front of tanks, as if it wasn't
the product of our own ridiculous safety.

Cocooned, and unembarrassed to be so
naive, so arrogant, to think we could bend

the world to our childish ideals.
What's the value of innocence

when the dream falls to the ground,
when you're stepping over the bodies of the dead?

What means your line in the sand,
when the sand is black with blood?

– when pacifism means helping the enemy?
– destruction, death, the wound unhealed?

As if you wouldn't weep for the heathen dead,
just boys and no more heathen than you or me

you softy. Weep and remember
love above all and put your war-boots on.

O bird
You beat the air so strongly with your wings
You make such an overwhelming
weather [
the power of
this wind . . .]
where have my ideas flown to?

From lines by Kenneth Patchen #42

The one we're really watching is Rishi Sunak,
the finance minister. Boris & Carrie Johnson
have paid their fines but as yet we've not heard anything
from Rishi Sunak, Chancellor of the Exchequer.

The first PM & Chancellor
to break the law in office:
when we're all in it together,
is this how you tell who the toff is?

The world is not so big when you think about it.
England is not so small. It's a non-dom rom-com.

You know a crook is what you are,
when you're grinning at the filling station
filling someone else's car,
evading your taxes in front of the nation.

& here's a fine pond for his wife to play Go Fishing
for slivers he's shaved off her taxes and the food banks.

'The guidelines were all followed;
there was never anything sinister'.
The one we're watching now
is that crooked finance minister.

'But' – the equally crooked PM explains,
as he lifts his pen to redact 'honesty'
and 'integrity' from the Ministerial Code –
'the people have a right to expect better'.

This government are cons and liars.
The public is aghast!

But Boris Johnson, who started the fires,
has spoken the truth at last.

[the lies the greed the lies & not at all
evil in any ultimate sense except]

From lines by Kenneth Patchen #43

A fiend slays the children of the messenger;
a minor fiend denies them lunch in school holidays.
Of course we understand they're poor in term-time, sure,

but they've always managed, in their eventfully mortal place,
to live somehow – who cares if they're as thin as reeds.

Come the day of rabblement, the rabble feeds.
A fiend will slay the messenger of the children's needs.
The children are too demoralised to run amok,

& in the meantime the party starts at seven sharp;
the piper's paid at midnight but nobody gives a fuck.

From lines by Kenneth Patchen #44

So tired of all this pathos, this emotion, all these
particulars, these sacred details like spots of blu-
tack left on the wall, all this clutter of feelings we
have to remember & all these faces, this human
dream! These granddads, all their passing smiles,
the letters they've read, their hopes for sun in the
morning or the innocent rain. Their roses. Oh but
everywhere you look some eventful, some heart-
sore moment, tiny throb of a vein at someone's
temple, a bluish inky letter to life itself – fleeing
highwayman who brings only destruction in the
end – he flashes like phosphorescence over the
town, the light falling like rain on the rooftops in
the village where under it nothing survives. Every
thing comes with a string attached & every string
is attached to something else, an endless chain
of colour & anti-colour & association & anti-matter
where nothing can just mean only itself pure, &
a butterfly lands on a rose, & a perfectly pleasant
rain that was meant to refresh granddad's roses –
those roses that were all that was left to him after

From lines by Kenneth Patchen #45

This darkness has lasted two months & today
is the summer solstice. The day of maximum
polarity: we're at our closest to the sun,
while the others are at their farthest possible
alienation. This darkness has been all mine,
nobody else needs to share in it.
I wander down the allotments: the only evil
is doubt, it's said, & I am made of it.
Show me my own name on a piece of paper
& I won't be sure. I look up everything these days.
Loose along its edges, close by the water,
I count a lot of blossoms. The allium,
an otherworldly purple pointillist globe
emerging from its garlic chrysalis.
The chamomile & roses, & the marigolds
& foxgloves, past which starving foxes run.
The darkness is all mine. 'The only evil
is doubt' – & even that's wrong. Manifold grasses
have grown knee-high under shaggy seedheads
they can barely support: spiky like wheat,
some rushy velvet. The pods, the burrs, the fronds.
I'm the one who's loose round the edges –
they don't sit by the pond & worry
whether they're good enough at being grass.
This world is finished, done.
& the sun sets blood-red on this, her day in the sun.

From lines by Kenneth Patchen #46

Days the anger leaves you &
there's no fight left, you're limp,
you're *untaut*, & who exactly do you
think you are anyway, what do you know
about anything – all those years, wasted
in *shitty, shitty England* – land of our bothers –
not being English, aping the betters all around you
so long you can't even claim to be a proper Yank any
more, that even worse imperialist. Fraud. Ignorant abroad.
You're flotsam, you've failed everybody: no one will take you
now for one of their own, you little broken sailboat with no sail,
floating loose in other people's waters, & all your crying little white-
eyed fishes. Ahhh the anger, I see it now, it's there but all turned against
yourself. Your solitude a dirty knife at your own throat. Well that's ok. Trust
has to be earned & you betray yourself with every breath, every word you utter,
every movement you commit. Stand up for yourself! You miserable little – Take
yourself seriously, whatever you are! You, you *woman*. Do some work for a change
& stop slacking with your total lack of authenticity, & behind with everything. It gets so
you can hardly shift out of bed some days, your mind is melted tar & your head's a bowl-
ing ball you can't lift much less throw at anyone – the dishes pile up in the sink, & the day
you try a selfie you don't know your own face. That 10,000-yard stare, that blank, paled-
out look of something dropped behind the couch <insert line from Kenneth Patchen here>

From lines by Kenneth Patchen #47

Joe Hill makes his way into the castle
through the silt of kings & queens.
He has never been here before but he hears
tell that there are flying monkeys.
They need him. He is interested in the silt –
grey, like ash, like the ashes of his brothers.
He is also interested in the gilt-
swagged mirror frames and interlaced
boughs and initials. *I bow to no man*,
he thinks, and knows these things, these
mere *things* are devoid
of meaning. In his right hand a kerchief
protects him from the silted-up
centuries of luxury & excess. From his left
spill a number of 5¢ picture postcards:
Park City, Utah, looking south, a mass
of jumbled dwellings, smokestack, mountains;
Mariinsky Hospital for the Poor, its gardens,
Dostoyevsky. Everything
has a meaning, as Joe Hill knows.
Everything is meaning. He is dying
for things that have no meaning but now
in this silted-up palace where he can't breathe,
in his soft haste he bumps
at the feet of the abyss. Nothing
has no meaning. *The King is Dead.*
And he, Joe Hill, is alive.
Alive, and he is wholly ghost.
Doesn't that mean something?

From lines by Kenneth Patchen #48

> . . . 'Yet there will be peace in certain
> parts of the city; sonnets dripping like moss from
> the walls; women holding their gifts out, arms,
> thighs, their quick song . . ..'
> — Kenneth Patchen, 'The Hunted City'

This body of blood & flesh, this 'gift',
this female body, about which even now so little is known
& so much contested
so many contracts drawn up by men –

it is the battleground
in every battle of your life –
a geography more advanced
than the most sophisticated cartographerman
just imagine victory in this war

if we are our bodies we have autonomy over them
if we have not autonomy over them we are not our bodies
in this case we exist as lifeless but sentient
entities roped to someone else's barrel
you could write a sonnet about this, maybe

From lines by Kenneth Patchen #49

1 Some rooms you have to climb up out of.
2 Blinding light as on the morning after when ice encases the branches like glass.
3 Metamorphosis I-V.
4 You never know what's been there in the night.
5 Beware men with braid on their shoulders.
6 Your friends are not always the ones you expected.
7 Whole villages.
8 A man sitting with his five small grandchildren, his sons & daughter dead.
9 Song of the blackbird.
10 Beware suburban arseholes dressed as shamans.
11 Chet's trumpet *is* his voice.
12 'For man himself is the door standing open to horror'.
13 'I have consulted the tribal books, the unpublished journals and the diaries'.
14 A dead crow cannot be any more beautiful.
15 'Put your helmet of steel on your head'.
16 Six dead in Fourth of July mass shooting.
17 Child crying.
18 The needed firepower has not arrived.
19 L'esprit d'escalier.
20 We are the richest generation who ever lived.
21 You can see that everybody is in shock.
22 Day after day, Schubert.
23 Summer whistles to her dogs of tree & flower', & carbon emission & riot.
24 1643: A group of disciplined pikemen standing their ground.
25 Mr Blackbird with his mouth full of grubs & worms.
26 Don't play in the boat.
27 'The stars tramp over heaven on their sticks' . . .
28 No; our grandparents were the richest generation who ever lived.
29 Scales, practised near a window over a garden.

30 The subject of every photograph is light.

31 Two shots in the back of the head.

32 'Thus I have learned to laugh & to grow roses in the black stone of the meeting halls.'

33 Puns about jazz: 'Ute be in England, now that spring is herr.'

34 While you are glamping, they are sitting in tents amid piles of rocks.

35 I have seen the lump of coal the Welsh coalworkers presented to their brother, Paul Robeson.

36 . . . pikemen standing their ground could be surprisingly effective.

37 I was wrong. I've always done this actually, Zoë.

38 Darkness whines outside the door to be let in.

39 The age at which Eric Ravilious died.

40 Snatches of wistful old songs waft across the rolling lawns, among flickers of indeterminate light.

41 Beware one magpie.

42 Scent of lily of the valley. Dotted swiss voile. Pink.

43 More ska, maybe.

From lines by Kenneth Patchen #50

i.m. Niall McDevitt and for James Byrne

Life! This terrible rotting, this
having-the-fruit & throwing it away,
this simple fear – the clinging, the cloying,

the cloaked, the choking – favourable
only to the most or the least exceptional –
& you don't know what kind of a thing

you are. & I don't know what kind
of thing I am [I'm here so far]. We find
out by being & then it's too late.

But you & I, we're in the same boat now,
rowing drunk, we're blindo, we're in
the same skin – we're all on our own –

& we all know, everybody knows, that
truth is always what they don't say. So
shut up, sing up, kiddos. What a revolution.

From lines by Kenneth Patchen #51

> *On alternating levels the world pounds in*
> *And there is not such another one anywhere.*
> > – Kenneth Patchen, 'The Overworld'

This town wakes up so early! sounds of the wood pigeons
cooing like a whisper of bells from the explosion-proofed church
with its openwork spire – & sleep never existed.

Crowds of sparrows shooting free of their warm trees
& along with the starlings thrushes get on with their tasks,
 killing their grubs & their sleepy snails.

The air foams with light – how naked & pink it is –
you could push tigers through these blushing bushes!
& forget the brides, Ken, your chivalry isn't wanted now.

Let the *women* quit wherever *we* have lain through the night,
haunting the places where the dead lie, dreaming of work,
dreaming of blood, & get on with our own tasks.

The dead don't mind us, we're just like them –
we feed our children & write our books. We have everything we need
to be at peace with the birds & the kids, & awake in the light.

Don't tell the horse that her rider can't hold the reins:
she doesn't care, she's running anyway. Don't talk about murder
to the man who has a knife in his back. Don't say STOP.

We all have a knife at our back. Dream easy, dream often.
And keep pushing those tigers through the flaming bushes:
what Stevens should have meant when he said red weather.

Source notes

Titles of poems by Kenneth Patchen from *Collected Poems*
(New York: New Directions, 1968)

#1   Portrait of the Artist as an Interior Decorator
#2   We Must Be Slow
       In a Crumbling
       I Feel Drunk All the Tine
       The Great Birds
       Soon it will
       Delighted with Bluepink
#3   Yesterday They Tried
       To Be Charmed
       Little Cannibal's Bedtimesong
#4   I Have No Place to Take Thee
       Latesummer Blues (In a Variety of Keys)
       Weekend Bathers
       THE STRANGE, MOVING LIGHTS OF PEOPLE . . .
#5   Should Be Sufficient
       Pick Up the Evening Paper
       And a Man Went Out Alone
#6   And the Sun Going Down
       Beyond the Dark Cedars
       The Origin of Baseball
       Beautiful You Are
#7   All the Flowery
       Do Me That Love
#8   The Bird-Queen
       Down in the Lone Valley
#9   The Continual Ministry of Thy Anger
       Where Every Prospect
       This Man Was Your Brother
#10   Cleveland, Oh?
       Joe Hill Listens to the Praying
       Kibali-Ituri
#11   There Are No Losses

Stayed No Longer in the Place Than to Hire a Guide for
        the Next Stage
Joe Hill Listens to the Praying
I Can't Understand! I Can't Understand!
#12 HARROWED BY THESE RESERVATIONS . . .
Written After Reading an Item in the Paper about a Young
        Lady Who Went Mad upon Forsaking Her Lover
You May All Go Home Now
The Spirit of Noplace
It Was a Bomby Evening
The Hunted City
The Forms of Knowledge
A SMALL BUT BRILLIANT FIRE GRAZED IN THE GRATE . . .
The Hunted City
O Howling Cells
#13 Two Ghosts Together
The Magical Mouse
Breathe on the Living
It Is for Us the Living
Investigation of Certain Interesting Questions
Biography of Southern Rain
All the Flowery
#14 The Origin of Baseball
The Lute in the Attic
The Hunted City
THE STRANGE, MOVING LIGHTS OF PEOPLE . . .
#15 The Middle Class was Sitting on Its Fat
This Man Was Your Brother
'Gentle and Giving' and Other Sayings
HARROWED BY THESE APPREHENSIONS . . .
He Thought of Mad Ellen's Ravings and of the Wretched
        Skeleton on the Rock
Always Another Viewpoint
A Man Lives Here
In Judgment of the Leaf
#16 Winter Poem
The Magic Car
An Easy Decision

This Summer Day

Can the Harp Shoot Through Its Propellers?

A Plate of Steaming Fish

#17   Boxers Hit Harder When Women Are Around

The New Being

'Gentle and Giving' and Other Sayings

Not If He Has Any Sense, He Won't Be Back

Beings So Hideous That the Air Weeps Blood

#18   The Orange Bears

Now If You

It's a Smallworld

And I, Too, Am Something of a Stranger Here, My Friend

Fog over the Sea and the Sun Going Down

Here Might Have Been the Thinking of Mountains

#19   The New Being

A Letter to the Inventors of a Tradition

#20   Childhood of the Hero

Opening the Window

#21   Thus Far So Nobly Advanced

The Question Is, Who Is Afraid of What?

The Manifold Fusions

The Orange Bears

O Fill Your Sack with Tiger Cubs

The Lute in the Attic

Poor Gorrel

Fields of Earth

Red Wine and Yellow Hair

#22   Old Man

At Grandmother's Wake

The Orange Bears

The Billion Freedoms

Dostoyevsky

#23   Like a Mourningless Child

#24   The Event at Konna

Old Man

The Stranger

It Depends on Whose Science

#25   At the Entrance to the Other World

'Gentle and Giving' and Other Sayings
Wouldn't You Be after a Jaunt of 964,000,000,000,000
   Million Miles?
The Origin of Baseball
The Little Black Train
It Depends on Whose Science
The Last Full Measure of Devotion
#26   The Grand Palace of Versialles
A Plate of Steaming Fish
#27   I Feel Drunk All the Time
We Mutually Pledge to Each Other
#28   A Fiend Slays the Children of the Messenger
Frogs and Queens
Childhood of the Hero
A Vanishing Unstituton
#29   No One Ever Works Alone
Death Will Amuse Them
Continuation of the Landscape
The Overworld
To Be Holy, Be Wholly Your Own
#30   'Gentle and Giving' and Other Sayings
This Early Day
It's Because Your Heart Is Pure, Honey
A Plate of Steaming Fish
#31   Among Ourselves and with All Nations
The Lute in the Attic
It's My Town!
The Hunted City
This Man Was Your Brother
Stayed No Longer in the Place Than to Hire a Guide for
   the Next Stage
#32   A Plate of Steaming Fish
This Summer Day
#33   Old Man
Backcountry Blues
The Little Black Train
#34   THE OLD LEAN OVER THE TOMBSTONES . . .
#35   Portrait of the Artist as an Interior Decorator

#36   Loyalty is the Life You Are
        Joe Hill Listens to the Praying
        The Lions of Fire Shall Have Their Hunting
#37   HARROWED BY THESE APPREHENSIONS . . .
        Street Corner College
#38   THE STRANGE, MOVING LIGHTS OF PEOPLE . . .
        Encounter at Nightfall
#39   A Man Lives Here
        Wanderers of the Pale Wood
        My Pretty Animals
        After an Old Song
#40   HARROWED BY THESE APPREHENSIONS . . .
        Joe Hill Listens to the Praying
        AVARICE AND AMBITION ONLY WERE THE FIRST BUILDERS . . .
        These Have Gone with Silent Hands, Seeking
        The First Crusades
        The Meaning of Life
#42   O My Love the Pretty Towns
#43   It Was a Bomby Evening
        Day of Rabblement
        The Intimate Guest
#45   So Be It
        The Rites of Darkness
        The Event at Konna
#46   Street Corner College
        The Lasting Seasons
#47   In the Fotsteps of the Walking Air
        AND HE HAD WILDER MOMENTS . . .
        Pleasures of This Gentle Day
        Kibali-Ituri
#49   The Hunted City
        O Everliving Queen!
#50   O What a Revolution
        An Old Pair of Shoes
        Old Man
        The New Being
#51   The Overworld

Acknowledgements

Poems from this collection have been published in the following magazines and webzines: *Blackbox Manifold*, *Ink Sweat and Tears*, *New Boots & Pantisocracies*, *Raceme* and *Shearsman*; on my Substack page *A Room of Someone Else's*; and attached to an essay on climate, capitalism and poetic resistance by Fran Lock on the *Culture Matters* website. An interview about this work appeared on the website of Leslie Tate, and another, with a poem, on the website of *Poetry Wales*.

No one writes a book alone.

I'd like to thank, wholeheartedly, the Royal Literary Fund, the Society of Authors, the Swale Borough Council benefits department, my GP, and everyone who paid me to do some work during this period.

Thanks to the London Writers' Salon with their online writing hours that literally got me out of bed and kept me out of it almost every day for a year.

We need our friends. Adam Horovitz, Natalia Zagorska-Thomas & Joe Furey were simply there, with Facetimes, Zoom calls, WhatsApps, sanity checks and artistic feedback. And thanks Joe for your amazing AI art. Geoff Sawers gave early feedback and made me a picture that says 'Fuck your Bunting'. The moral support of Fran Lock meant the world. Thanks Tony Street just for being you. And Fran Sexton, and Vanessa Claridge. David Secombe. Nora Meyer. Plus hundreds of Facebook friends, who are a real ecosystem. My family, from afar. And thanks to my kids, who aren't kids any more, & my kids-in-law – Em, Nat, Daisy, Sophie & Adam, & little Nylah – for being *actually* the world.

editions

Founded in 2007, CB editions publishes chiefly short
fiction and poetry, including work in translation.

Books can be ordered from www.cbeditions.com.